# Nonfiction Classics for Students, Volume 3

*Staff*

**Editor:** Jennifer Smith.

**Contributing Editors:** Anne Marie Hacht, Michael L. LaBlanc, Ira Mark Milne, Daniel Toronto, Carol Ullmann.

**Managing Editor, Content:** Dwayne D. Hayes.

**Managing Editor, Product:** David Galens.

**Publisher, Literature Product:** Mark Scott.

**Literature Content Capture:** Joyce Nakamura, *Managing Editor*. Sara Constantakis, *Editor*.

**Research:** Victoria B. Cariappa, *Research Manager*. Sarah Genik, Tamara Nott, Tracie A. Richardson, *Research Associates*. Nicodemus Ford, *Research Assistant*.

**Permissions:** Maria L. Franklin, *Permissions Manager*. Shalice Shah-Caldwell, *Permissions*

*Associate.* Debra Freitas, *IC Coordinator/Permissions Associate.*

**Manufacturing:** Mary Beth Trimper, *Manager, Composition and Electronic Prepress.* Evi Seoud, *Assistant Manager, Composition Purchasing and Electronic Prepress.* Stacy Melson, *Buyer.*

**Imaging and Multimedia Content Team:** Barbara Yarrow, *Manager.* Randy Bassett, *Imaging Supervisor.* Robert Duncan, Dan Newell, Luke Rademacher, *Imaging Specialists.* Leitha Etheridge-Sims, Mary Grimes, David G. Oblender, *Image Catalogers.* Robyn V. Young, *Project Manager.* Dean Dauphinais, *Senior Image Editor.* Kelly A. Quin, *Image Editor.*

**Product Design Team:** Pamela A. E. Galbreath, *Senior Art Director.* Michael Logusz, *Graphic Artist.*

## *Copyright Notice*

Since this page cannot legibly accommodate all copyright notices, the acknowledgments constitute an extension of the copyright notice.

While every effort has been made to secure permission to reprint material and to ensure the reliability of the information presented in this publication, Gale neither guarantees the accuracy of the data contained herein nor assumes any responsibility for errors, omissions, or discrepancies. Gale accepts no payment for listing; and inclusion in the publication of any organization, agency, institution, publication, service, or individual does not imply endorsement of the editors or publisher. Errors brought to the attention of the publisher and verified to the satisfaction of the publisher will be corrected in future editions.

This publication is a creative work fully protected by all applicable copyright laws, as well as by misappropriation, trade secret, unfair competition, and other applicable laws. The authors and editors of this work have added value to the underlying factual material herein through one or more of the following: unique and original selection, coordination, expression, arrangement, and classification of the information.

All rights to this publication will be vigorously defended.

Copyright © 2002

The Gale Group
27500 Drake Road
Farmington Hills, MI 48331-3535

All rights reserved including the right of reproduction in whole or in part in any form.

ISBN 0-7876-5453-1
ISSN 1533-7561
Printed in the United States of America.

10 9 8 7 6 5 4 3 2 1

# *Backlash: The Undeclared War Against American Women*

## Susan Faludi
## 1991

## Introduction

Susan Faludi's bestselling book, *Backlash: The Undeclared War Against American Women*, is a methodically researched and documented work challenging conventional wisdom about the American women's movement and women's gains in achieving equality in the latter years of the twentieth century. Faludi begins the book by looking carefully at then-current myths about the status of women, including the press reports that single career women are more likely to be depressed than other women, that professional women are leaving their jobs in droves to stay at home, and that single working women over age thirty have a small chance of ever getting married. Not only are these myths not true, says Faludi, but they are evidence of a society-wide backlash against women and what they have achieved in recent years. She describes this backlash as a "kind of pop-culture version of the Big Lie" and declares that "it stands the truth boldly on its head and proclaims that the very steps that have elevated women's positions have actually led to their downfall."

In her book, Faludi takes the press to task for failing to challenge the myths about women in the 1980s and especially for spreading, through "trend journalism," stories about how unhappy women are, despite their having reaped the benefits of women's liberation in the 1970s. Faludi challenges the prevailing wisdom that the women's movement is to blame for women's unhappiness; she believes their unhappiness actually stems from the fact that the struggle for equality is not yet finished.

Faludi uses data from a wide variety of sources, such as government and university studies, newspapers, census reports, scholarly journals, and personal interviews to explore women's status in the 1980s. The personal interviews offer a look at the individuals who are behind the "backlash" and, according to Faludi, are hindering women's progress.

## Author Biography

Susan Faludi was born in New York City on April 18, 1959 to Steven Faludi, a photographer, and Marilyn Lanning Faludi, an editor. When Faludi's *Backlash: The Undeclared War Against American Women* was released in 1991, the book received honors and postive and negative criticism for its controversial content. Susan Faludi, however, was already familiar with controversy. Faludi covered a number of contentious subjects for her high school and college newspapers. Writing for her high school newspaper, she addressed the issue of whether several on-campus Christian organizations had violated the concept of the separation of church and state. While an undergraduate at Harvard University, she wrote an article on sexual harassment that led to the dismissal of a guilty professor after the article was published.

After graduating from Harvard, Faludi worked for the *New York Times,* the *Miami Herald,* and the *Atlanta Constitution* and soon garnered a reputation as a crusading journalist. She received a 1991 Pulitzer Prize for an article she wrote for the *Wall Street Journal* on the Safeway Stores' leveraged buyout and its impact on employees.

In 1986, Faludi contacted the U. S. Census Bureau about the notorious Harvard-Yale marriage study and discovered that the study's methodology and results—including the much-quoted finding that single, educated, career women over thirty had only a 20 percent chance of ever getting married—were suspect. Though she and other writers reported the errors in the study, most of the national press simply focused on the sensational results. Faludi's interest in discerning the facts from the fictions about women's status in the 1980s prompted her to write *Backlash: The Undeclared War Against American Women*.

The book went on to win the National Book Critics Circle Award for Nonfiction in 1991. Since then, Faludi has written for various periodicals, including *Mother Jones* and *Ms.* In 1999, she published her second book, *Stiffed: The Betrayal of the American Man*, a similarly extensive tome on issues American men are feeling. Faludi currently lives and writes in California.

# Plot Summary

## *Chapter One*

Faludi begins by stating that, though many may agree that the end of the twentieth century is a good time to be a woman, press reports and surveys indicate that women are unhappy with their lives. Often, this is blamed on a variety of factors related to feminism, such as women working outside the home. "Women are enslaved by their own liberation," claim many commentators who argue against feminism. But Faludi disagrees, arguing instead that women are unhappy because the real work of achieving equality has barely begun. She uses statistics that show that women still make less money and hold more low-status jobs than men and that domestic violence and rape are on the rise:

> The truth is that the last decade has seen a powerful counterassault on women's rights, a backlash, an attempt to retract the handful of small and hard-won victories the feminist movement did manage to win for women.

## *Chapter Two*

Faludi presents a number of what she calls myths, stories "that have supported the backlash against women's quest for equality." Even though these myths have appeared in newspapers and have become accepted facts in America, they are untrue. These myths include the notions that women are finding it more difficult to find husbands, that no-fault divorce laws are to blame for the reduction in the standard of living of divorced women, that professional women are increasingly infertile, that career women have more mental illnesses than noncareer women, and that children in day care suffer permanent damage.

## *Chapter Three*

The history of women's rights in the United States is much longer than most people believe, Faludi says, and dates to well before the 1970s, a decade that many today see as the advent of feminism. While backlashes against women's rights can be traced to colonial times, Faludi limits her examination to the backlashes after the four most recent periods of advancement: the mid-nineteenth century, the early 1900s, the early 1940s, and the early 1970s. Currently, she says, Americans are in a backlash phase against the advances made in the 1970s. She also notes that each of the backlash periods included a supposed "crisis in masculinity" and its companion, "a call to femininity."

## *Chapter Four*

This chapter covers how the media, through "trend journalism," helped create the backlash against women's rights and feminism in the 1980s by coining the terms "mommy track," "biological clock," and "man shortage." The press sought to answer the question of why women, after years of advances, still felt dissatisfied. Their answer was that feminism's achievements, not society's "resistance to these partial achievements," were causing the stress among women. The media claimed that there was a trend afoot (personified in the "New Traditionalist" woman) in which women were choosing home life over careers; this did not have any statistical support, according to Faludi. Media reports were presenting a view of single women as defective, while single men were lauded for making "mature" decisions.

## *Chapter Five*

Here, Faludi addresses how the backlash shaped Hollywood's portrayal of women in the 1980s. While a number of films in the 1970s positively portrayed single women making choices that supported their careers, the 1980s produced a crop of films in which single career women were made to pay dearly for their decisions not to have children and husbands. Faludi points to *Fatal Attraction* as the epitome of anti-feminism in the late 1980s. In the movie, Glenn Close plays a bitter, single, career woman who takes out her anger on otherwise happily married Michael Douglas after a brief affair. In many 1980s films, as in *Fatal Attraction,* Faludi states, the plot involves the feminine "Light Woman" killing the aggressively manly "Dark Woman." The press, however, declared that these movies' themes constituted a trend and found actual women like Close's character to write about.

## Chapter Six

According to Faludi, while women largely disappeared from prime-time television programming in the late 1980s (as they did in the late 1950s and early 1960s), "TV's counterassault on women's liberation would be … more restrained than Hollywood's." During the mid-1970s, many television series tackled political issues, including feminism. But by the early 1980s, the tide was beginning to turn. The few shows with strong women were toned down to appeal to advertisers. Television in the 1980s condemned women who dared step outside the home, and single career women were usually given angry or neurotic personalities. The only "good" female character in the popular series *thirtysomething* was the angelic Hope, according to Faludi, a stay-at-home mom who was the envy of her careerist female friends.

## Chapter Seven

In the 1970s, the fashion industry responded to a push from career women to produce more suits and practical clothing. But in the 1980s, a backlash occurred in which designers decided that fashion would be more feminine and fantastical—even to the point of childishness. One of the chief perpetrators of this "little girl" look was Christian Lacroix, according to Faludi. After a lull in the 1970s in sales of undergarments and lingerie, the industry declared that the 1980s was seeing a boom in this area. However, according to Faludi, this was a press-generated trend and did not reflect reality. A major reason women were not buying lingerie was that the styles in the late 1980s "celebrated the repression, not the flowering of female sexuality."

## *Chapter Eight*

In the 1980s, the beauty industry—including those who encouraged unnecessary plastic surgery as well as those who sold cosmetics—set a standard of femininity for American women that Faludi believes was "grossly unnatural." Even though it may be one of the most superficial of the cultural institutions involved in the backlash, Faludi believes that, because the beauty industry changed how women felt about themselves, it was the most destructive.

## *Chapter Nine*

Faludi discusses the "New Right movement" of the 1980s and its agenda—purported to be profamily but, in her opinion, was simply anti-women and anti-feminist. Faludi focuses on the women who work for New Right organizations, such as the Heritage Foundation and Concerned Women for America. She notes that even though these organizations claim that women cannot be both good mothers and good career women, the New Right's female leaders are living lives that contradict this sentiment.

## *Chapter Ten*

Ronald Reagan's election to the presidency in 1980 came with the help of many New Right women, Faludi asserts. However, she notes that a by-product of Reagan's victory was that "women began disappearing from federal office"—even women who were conservative and anti-feminist. Faludi adds that Democrats did much the same thing during the 1980s and that no one challenged them.

## *Chapter Eleven*

Faludi argues that "the backlash's emissaries" came not only from the New Right movement but also from among the numerous writers, scholars, and thinkers who appeared in the mainstream media. In this chapter, she profiles nine of these men and women, not in an attempt to "psychoanalyze" them, she says, but to offer an overview of those who helped make the backlash against women's rights more "palatable for public consumption." They include George Gilder, Allan Bloom, Michael and Margarita Levin, Warren Farrell, Robert Bly, Sylvia Ann Hewlett, Betty Friedan, and Carol Gilligan.

## *Chapter Twelve*

In the 1970s, according to Faludi, commercially popular therapeutic and self-help books directed toward women told their readers that they had the right to be treated with respect. In contrast, similar books published in the 1980s urged women to keep quiet and not challenge the social order. These books also blamed feminism for women's unhappiness and asked their readers to criticize only themselves if their lives were not what they envisioned. Meanwhile, the American Psychological Association amended its standard diagnosis reference to include, according to Faludi, anti-woman definitions for two disorders, masochistic personality disorder and pre-menstrual syndrome.

## *Chapter Thirteen*

The Reagan administration in the 1980s downplayed reports that women were losing status in the workplace, according to Faludi. The press failed to investigate this disinformation campaign and actually participated in publicizing misinformation about the backlash against working women. After the gains made in the 1970s, women particularly in the media, retail, and blue-collar industries suffered in their efforts to secure workplace equality in the 1980s.

## *Chapter Fourteen*

In this chapter, Faludi discusses how the 1980s backlash against women affected their reproductive rights. In 1973, the U. S. Supreme Court declared abortion legal in *Roe v. Wade,* but during the 1980s organizations such as Operation Rescue and many conservative politicians wanted to reverse the result of the ruling. Faludi argues that women's ability to regulate their fertility contributed to dramatic changes "not in the abortion rate but in female sexual behavior and attitudes," and this was frightening to many. According to Faludi, in the 1980s, women were losing the right to make decision regarding the treatment of their bodies while pregnant.

## *Epilogue*

Faludi tells a number of women's personal stories to show that "for all the forces the backlash mustered ... women never really surrendered." She is, though, somewhat disappointed that women as a whole did not take advantage of their numbers as much as they could have in the 1980s to make their case for equality. "The '80s could have become American women's great leap forward," she believes.

# Key Figures

## *Neil Bennett*

Neil Bennett was one of the researchers involved in the 1986 Harvard-Yale marriage study, which concluded that college-educated, never-married women past the age of thirty had a slim chance of ever marrying. Bennett was a Yale University sociologist when stories about the as-yet-unpublished study on women's marriage patterns ran in various media outlets. This study generated the idea that there was a "man shortage" in America, something Faludi denies in her book.

## *Allan Bloom*

Allan Bloom was a professor at the University of Chicago and writer of the bestselling book *The Closing of the American Mind.* While the book has been publicized as a treatise on education, Faludi argues that it was actually "an assault on the women's movement." According to Faludi, Bloom believes that "most faculty jobs and publication rights are now reserved for feminist women" and that women who try to mix a career with rearing children are hurting their families.

## *David Bloom*

David Bloom was one of the researchers involved in the 1986 Harvard-Yale marriage study, which claimed that college-educated, never-married women past the age of thirty had a small chance of ever marrying. Bloom was a Harvard economist when stories about the as-yet-unpublished study on women's marriage patterns ran in various media outlets. This study generated the idea that there was a "man shortage" in America, something Faludi denies in her book.

## *Robert Bly*

Originally a poet and Vietnam-era anti-war activist, Robert Bly re-created himself in the 1980s as a leader in what Faludi calls "the men's movement." This movement, according to Faludi, was based upon the idea that men were becoming "soft" and were out of touch with their masculinity. "In short," she writes, "the Great Mother's authority has become too great." Across the country, Bly held weekend retreats in the woods devoted to reconnecting men with their masculinity through drumming and Native American rituals.

## *Diana Doe*

Diana Doe is a pseudonym for a thirty-five-year-old single, working woman who, though she was a public figure, asked Faludi not to use her real name in the book. Doe bet a doubtful male colleague—who had called her "physically inferior" to younger women—that she would be married by the time she was forty despite press reports in 1986 stating that professional single women over thirty had a 5 percent chance of ever marrying. To help her chances of marriage, Doe decided to get a complete physical makeover through plastic surgery and other techniques. She created a market plan in which she agreed to sell the story of her physical "metamorphosis" to various media outlets and gave herself a stage name: "the Ultimate Five Percent Woman." The "project," as Doe referred to it, required her to mention the names of her plastic surgeon, dentist, exercise trainer, and beautician in articles and during personal appearances in exchange for their services. During the project, Doe appeared on a radio show and received criticism from male listeners who considered her vain and unnatural. Faludi bemoans the case of Doe, noting that first a male colleague criticized her for not being young, and then "men were criticizing her for trying to live up to male-created standards—standards she had made her own."

## *Greg Duncan*

Greg Duncan was a University of Michigan social scientist working with Saul Hoffman. They challenged Marlene Weitzman's argument that divorce was impoverishing women. Duncan used his and Hoffman's research and Weitzman's numbers to conclude that, while women did suffer a drop in their standard of living after divorce, that drop was temporary. According to Duncan and his research partner, women's living standards five years after a divorce were actually higher than they had been before the divorce.

## *Warren Farrell*

As a young academic, Warren Farrell supported the women's movement, writing the "celebrated male feminist tome" *The Liberated Man,* and founding some sixty men's chapters of the National Organization for Women. But by the mid-1980s, Farrell decided that men were more oppressed than women and wrote *Why Men Are the Way They Are,* in which he argued that women had been venting too much anger at men and had exerted too much power over them. He taught classes on men's issues at the University of California School of Medicine at San Diego.

## *Geraldine Ferraro*

Geraldine Ferraro was a member of Congress when Democrat Walter Mondale selected her to be his vice presidential running mate in 1984. Faludi notes that Ferraro's nomination provoked attacks from many conservative politicians and notions that the Democrats had "surrendered" to feminists by choosing her.

## *Betty Freidan*

Betty Freidan was once one of America's most famous feminists, a founder of the National Organization for Women and author of the groundbreaking 1963 book, *The Feminine Mystique.* Faludi writes about Freidan's 1981 book, *The Next Stage,* which argues that the leaders of the women's movement in the 1960s and 1970s had ignored the issues of motherhood and family and had been too confrontational.

## *George Gilder*

George Gilder initially supported feminism and women's rights, according to Faludi, but ultimately made a name for himself as a conservative media commentator and writer. In his words, he decided to become "America's number-one antifeminist" by writing such books as *Wealth and Poverty, Sexual Suicide, Men and Marriage,* and *Naked Nomads.*

## *Carol Gilligan*

Many books were published in the 1980s on how women are different from men and about "women's inordinate capacity for kindness, service to others, and cooperation," according to Faludi. During this period, Carol Gilligan wrote *In a Different Voice,* a book Faludi refers to as "one of the most influential feminist works of the '80s." While Gilligan wrote the book to illustrate how men diminished women's moral development, the book was misinterpreted by antifeminist groups to support discriminatory practices against women.

## *Sylvia Ann Hewlett*

Sylvia Ann Hewlett, a member of the Council on Foreign Relations and other think-tanks, indicted the women's movement in her book *A Lesser Life: Myths of Women's Liberation in America.* The book argued that, while feminism may be helpful to upper-class career women, it is actually harmful to what she calls "ordinary women."

## Media Adaptations

- Susan Faludi is the reader on the audiotape version of her book, *Backlash: The Undeclared War against American Women.* Publishing Mills produced the audiotape in 1992.

## *Saul Hoffman*

Saul Hoffman was a University of Delaware

economist who specialized in divorce statistics and worked with Greg Duncan. They challenged Marlene Weitzman's argument that divorce was impoverishing women, using their own research and Weitzman's numbers. They discovered that, while women did suffer a drop in their standard of living after divorce, that drop was temporary. According to Hoffman and Duncan, women's living standards five years after a divorce were actually higher than they had been before the divorce.

## *Christian Lacroix*

Christian Lacroix was a fashion designer. Faludi writes that Lacroix launched a look called "High Femininity," in which women's bodies were cinched into waist-pinching corsets and reshaped by push-up bras. In his own words, Lacroix created these clothes for women who like to "dress up like little girls." Lacroix and other designers participated in the backlash against feminism by promoting "punitively restrictive clothing," according to Faludi.

## *Beverly LaHaye*

Beverly LaHaye was an example of a paradox for Faludi: a high-powered career woman with a family and yet a supporter of the New Right's conviction that such a life is neither possible nor appropriate. LaHaye founded the antifeminist organization Concerned Women for America in 1978. In Faludi's book, LaHaye claims that her power and authority did not contradict the concept that men should be the heads of households, as women like her were only seeking "spiritual power" and not earthly power. LaHaye wrote a book outlining this philosophy, *The Spirit-Controlled Woman* and also wrote *The Act of Marriage: The Beauty of Sexual Love,* a book Faludi calls "the evangelical equivalent of *The Joy of Sex.*"

## *Sherry Lansing*

Sherry Lansing was a movie executive responsible for releasing films such as *Fatal Attraction* and *The Accused* in the 1980s. Faludi points to *Fatal Attraction,* the story of a single career woman whose affair with a married man sparks her obsession with him, as part of the evidence of a societal and cultural backlash against women's rights in the 1980s. According to Faludi, Lansing's release of *The Accused,* a film about a woman who is gang-raped while a group of men stand by but don't interfere was a feeble attempt to "polish up her feminist credentials." Faludi questions whether audiences needed to be "reminded that rape victims deserve sympathy."

## *Margarita Levin*

Margarita Levin was a philosophy professor at Yeshiva University, with a specialty in the philosophy of mathematics. She was also, according to Faludi, "an intellectual partner" in her husband, Michael Levin's, "antifeminist writings." Faludi reports that, ironically, many of the typically female jobs in the Levin household, such as child care, were done by Michael Levin as well as by his wife.

## *Michael Levin*

Michael Levin was a philosophy professor who wrote *Feminism and Freedom,* a book arguing that sex roles are innate and that women who attempt to have both family and career are denying these sex roles. He was married to Margarita Levin, also a philosophy professor. Faludi reports that many of the typically female jobs in the Levin household, such as child care, were done by Michael Levin as well as by his wife.

## *Adrian Lyne*

Adrian Lyne directed the 1987 blockbuster movie *Fatal Attraction,* in which a single career woman has an affair with a married man and stalks him after he tries to break off the relationship. Faludi points to this movie as part of the evidence of a societal and cultural backlash against women's rights in the 1980s. She highlights Lyne's role in turning the character of the single woman into "the Dark Woman." According to Faludi, Lyne once commented that unmarried women are "sort of overcompensating for not being men."

## *John T. Malloy*

John Malloy, a former English teacher, wrote

the 1977 bestselling book *The Woman's Dress for Success Book.* The book encouraged women to dress for the jobs they wanted. Faludi notes that Malloy was "an advocate for women's rising expectations—and urged them to rely on their brains rather than their bodies to improve their station." She argues that much of the "High Femininity" fashion look of the 1980s was a backlash against what Malloy stood for.

## *Paul Marciano*

Paul Marciano, along with his brothers, created the Guess line of jeans and clothing in the early 1980s. Faludi asserts that Guess found a way to "use the backlash to sell clothes" by developing an ad campaign featuring passive-looking women with strong-looking men. Marciano claimed that the design of the ads reflected his love of the American West and the 1950s, places and periods in which women, he said, "know their place, which is supportive, and their function, which is decorative."

## *Connie Marshner*

Connie Marshner was an executive with the conservative organizations Free Congress Research and Education Foundation and the Heritage Foundation. She was the child of liberal parents who encouraged her to go to school and have a career. Faludi draws a profile of her as a woman who has been helped by feminism—she has had a thriving and powerful career as well as a family—

and yet still supports the New Right thinking that a woman cannot have a career and be a mother.

## *Jeanne Moorman*

Jeanne Moorman, a demographer in the marriage and family statistics branch of the U. S. Census Bureau, heard about the Harvard-Yale marriage study from the numerous reporters who called her looking for a comment on it. Moorman attempted to reproduce the survey's results. According to her calculations, the likelihood that college-educated, never-wed women past the age of thirty would marry was considerably greater than the Harvard-Yale study had concluded. Her findings showed that these women were simply getting married later in life, not failing to marry. Moorman's attempts to contact the researchers at Yale and Harvard were ignored at first. When they finally did respond, the researchers were uncooperative and difficult, according to Faludi.

## *Faith Popcorn*

Faith Popcorn was an advertising executive and "leading consumer authority" who became well known in the 1980s for predicting social trends. She admitted that her predictions often came from popular magazines, television shows, and bestselling books, rather than from consumer research. Popcorn predicted that "cocooning" was the major national trend for the 1980s, meaning that people were becoming more interested in staying home and eating "Mom foods" such as meatloaf and chicken potpie. Faludi argues that, while Popcorn may have intended for cocooning to be a "gender neutral concept, the press made it a female trend, defining cocooning not as *people* coming home but as *women* abandoning the office."

## *Ronald Reagan*

Ronald Reagan was elected United States president in 1980 on a conservative social and economic platform. Faludi notes that in a 1982 speech he blamed working women for the tight job market. Reagan said in the speech that high unemployment figures were related to "the increase in women who are working today."

## *Charles Revson*

Charles Revson was the head of Revlon, a cosmetics company. In the early 1970s, he came up with the idea of creating a perfume for women that would celebrate women's liberation and independence. The perfume, Charlie, was a huge success. By the late 1980s, however, the marketing campaign for Charlie was modified, according to a Revson spokesperson, to reflect that "we had gone a little too far with the whole women's liberation thing."

## *Phyllis Schlafly*

Phyllis Schlafly was a part of the conservative

New Right political movement in the 1980s. She campaigned against the Equal Rights Amendment (ERA) to the U. S. Constitution. Schlafly was a Harvard-educated lawyer, author of numerous books, and two-time congressional candidate who fought against the ERA because, in Schlafly's words, "it would take away the marvelous legal rights of a woman to be a fulltime wife and mother in the house supported by her husband."

## *Aaron Spelling*

Aaron Spelling was the producer behind the late 1980s television series *Angels '88,* a reprise of his earlier series *Charlie's Angels,* in which, according to Faludi, "three jiggle-prone private eyes took orders from invisible boss Charlie and bounced around in bikinis." Spelling assured the press that his new show was much more advanced than *Charlie's Angels* because the women's boss was a female nurse.

## *Ben Wattenberg*

Ben Wattenberg was a syndicated columnist, senior fellow at the American Enterprise Institute, and author of the 1987 book *The Birth Dearth.* In the book, Wattenberg introduced the concept that American women's decisions to have fewer children would hurt the nation's economy and culture. According to Faludi, Wattenberg and others were urging women to have children based on "society's baser instincts—xenophobia, militarism, and bigotry" by arguing that if white, educated, middle-class women didn't have babies, "paupers, fools and foreigners would." Wattenberg blamed the women's movement and feminism for discouraging women from their more traditional societal roles.

## *Lenore Weitzman*

Lenore Weitzman wrote the 1985 book *The Divorce Revolution: The Unexpected Social and Economic Consequences for Women and Children in America.* According to Faludi, Weitzman's thesis, that the recent no-fault divorce laws in America were systematically impoverishing divorced women and their children, increased the "attack on divorce-law reform" in the 1980s. While Weitzman herself never blamed feminists for no-fault divorce legislation, Faludi notes that those who were promoting and supporting her book did so.

## *Paul Weyrich*

Paul Weyrich, head of the Free Congress Research and Education Foundation, is considered by many to be the "Father of the New Right." The New Right was the conservative political movement that supported Ronald Reagan in the early 1980s and put many conservative Republicans in Congress. In Faludi's book, Weyrich called the late 1980s a period when "women are discovering they can't have it all" and that having a career will destroy their family life. He also said that the New Right movement was different from other conservative movements in that it did not want simply to "preserve the status quo" but to "overturn the present power structure of the country." One of the major pieces of legislation he supported at the beginning of the 1980s was the Family Protection Act, which, according to Faludi, was intended to eliminate federal laws supporting equal education.

## Themes

## *Structure and Functioning of Families*

Conservative thinkers and writers object to feminism because it ignores what they see as a woman's natural inclination toward making a home for her children and husband. In their eyes, feminists' endorsement of a woman's ability to maintain a home while pursuing a career threatens the family structure by subverting the man as the traditional head of the household. This, in turn, threatens the country's social and economic structure. Those who view feminism in this way believe that the women's movement is not only encouraging women to work while they have children but also to forgo or delay having children. Faludi is particularly concerned that the backlash against women delaying childbirth encourages press reports that there is an "epidemic" of infertility among career women.

Some conservative commentators, who argue that feminists have encouraged women to remain childless, believe that such urgings place the nation at an economic disadvantage in the world. In her analysis of this argument, Faludi asserts that those who make this case for American women having children can be accused of racism and xenophobia. She believes that they are worried not only about

America's economic future but also about the possibility of whites becoming a minority among people of color and foreigners.

Faludi delights in revealing the personal lives of many of the conservative thinkers who oppose feminism, observing that those lives very often run counter to the tenets of their public comments. She writes about a number of the women involved in the New Right who, despite their arguments that careers and motherhood do not mix, are pursuing lives filled with both children and work. She also points out the number of men in these prominent couples who take over the household duties, such as child care and cooking, so that their wives can pursue careers.

## *Popular Culture in the 1980s*

Faludi uses popular culture during the 1980s to buttress her argument that the decade was a period of backlash against women and feminism. Her evidence for this backlash includes examples from the movie industry, television, the cosmetics and beauty industry, the fashion world, and societal trends.

For example, Faludi notes that after a decade filled with television series like *All in the Family,* which tackled tough political issues (including women's rights), television in the mid-to late 1980s featured few programs in which women's issues were considered. The rare 1980s show featuring a strong woman was usually under threat of cancellation. In the movies, women were regularly beaten, pitted against each other, or punished for being single. Hollywood supported the backlash by showing American women who were "unhappy because they were too free [and] their liberation had denied them marriage and motherhood," says Faludi. The fashion industry reinforced the backlash, as well, by designing clothing that was either childlike or extremely restrictive and binding.

## *The Struggle for Equal Rights*

Faludi's book is concerned with a period in history—the 1980s—during which women's struggle for equal rights suffered setbacks. She notes, however, that these periods of backlash historically occur after periods of advancement in women's rights. According to Faludi, the mid-nineteenth century, the early 1900s, the early 1940s, and the early 1970s were eras during which American women saw large gains in their economic and social status. "In each case, the struggle yielded to backlash," asserts Faludi.

Faludi points out that the backlash against women is cyclical. For example, when she speaks of movies in the 1980s, she also looks at the tenor of movies in the 1970s. When she examines 1980s fashions, she also considers what women were wearing in the 1950s, a period of backlash after the advances of the 1940s.

# Topics for Further Study

- Susan Faludi wrote her book primarily in the late 1980s. Do you think the status of women in the United States has changed since then? What about societal attitudes? Is society in a period of backlash or of advancement for women's rights? Provide specific examples from some of the sectors of society covered in Faludi's book—the entertainment industry, the media, government, and so forth—to support your opinion.

- Faludi mentions quite a few movies as evidence that a backlash against women occurred in the 1980s. Watch one of the movies she says is anti-feminist and write a short essay agreeing or disagreeing with her position. Use specific examples from the movie to make your argument. Has she misinterpreted this movie or is she correct in her evaluation?

- Research the four periods of American history during which Faludi says there were advancements in the status of women. Also research the years following these periods, when Faludi argues that there was backlash against women. Create a time line for each of these advancement and backlash eras, including both events pertaining to women's rights and unrelated national and world events. Analyze and explain any patterns you see.

- Interview a woman you know who has a career and is also a mother. Ask her questions about some of the issues explored in *Backlash*. Choose your questions based on the issues you find most interesting. Then write up your interview in the form of a newspaper feature article.

- Choose someone Faludi interviewed for her book and do research to find out what that person is doing now and whether his or her views have changed.

## *Myths and Their Role in Society*

Faludi points out that many in society, including some well-meaning writers and thinkers, have accepted the truth of myths about the status of women in the 1980s. She exposes many of these myths and supposed trends, which have appeared so often in the press that most Americans consider them as fact. For example, Faludi discovered that the Harvard-Yale marriage study, proclaiming that unmarried women after the age of thirty have a very slim chance of ever becoming wed was full of methodological errors. She also challenges stories claiming that single career women suffer from depression in epidemic numbers.

# Style

## *Use of Evidence to Make an Argument*

Faludi's book is overflowing with data and information that she believes bolsters her case that the 1980s represented a period of backlash against women and their advances. Her supporting data comes from a wide variety of sources, including newspapers, scholarly and academic journals, personal interviews, and government and university studies. This use of authoritative sources is an important way writers convince readers of their argument; however, some critics have suggested that Faludi uses almost too much factual data and that its volume actually hinders her argument.

## *Personal Profiles*

Faludi also includes short profiles of people she believes were critical to the evolution of the backlash against women in the 1980s. Inclusion of these profiles helps move the book along in a number of ways: reading about specific individuals who contributed to the backlash—even though Faludi obviously disagrees with their philosophy—puts a human face on the philosophy and makes the issues seem less amorphous; and the profiles offer some relief from the pages and pages of data. Faludi is able to point her finger directly at the commentators, writers, politicians, and thinkers who she feels helped the backlash gain momentum.

# Historical Context

## *The Equal Rights Amendment*

Despite the apparent simplicity of the language in the proposed Equal Rights Amendment (ERA) to the U. S. Constitution, it was one of the most divisive political issues in the 1970s. The fifty-two words of the amendment were as follows:

> 1. Equality of rights under the law shall not be denied or abridged by the United States or by any State on account of sex. 2. The Congress shall have the power to enforce, by appropriate legislation, the provisions of this article. 3. This amendment shall take effect two years after the date of ratification.

The issue of an equal rights amendment to the U. S. Constitution first emerged in the 1920s and appeared on a regular basis thereafter. Early opponents to the amendment—including labor unions and social reform groups—cited uncertainty about how the proposal would affect legislation meant to assist women and children. In 1972, the U. S. Congress passed the ERA. The next step was for the legislatures of thirty-eight states (three-fourths of the fifty states) to ratify the amendment by 1979. In about a year, twenty-five states had passed the ERA.

The pace of ratification then slowed tremendously. In 1977, only three more states were needed for the amendment to become part of the U. S. Constitution, but by the 1979 deadline this had not happened. Congress extended the deadline to 1982, but no other states ratified the ERA after 1977, and the amendment failed.

Opposition to the ERA came primarily from political conservatives who feared that the amendment would substantially change the roles of men and women. Phyllis Schlafly, a conservative activist, organized the Stop ERA campaign, based primarily on the issue of the amendment's impact on families. She and others argued that the ERA would bring an end to a husband's obligation to support his wife and children, force the creation of unisex bathrooms, and include women in the military draft.

## *Abortion Rights*

Faludi points out that American women's access to legal abortion was generally uncontested until the last half of the nineteenth century. By the end of the nineteenth century, every state in the union had outlawed abortion except in cases in which the woman's life was in jeopardy. In 1967, the National Organization for Women advocated the repeal of abortion laws, and other organizations, such as the group Zero Population Growth, also saw access to abortion as part of their agendas. By 1969, the National Association for the Repeal of Abortion Laws (NARAL) was founded. NARAL made progress organizing at the state level and had received qualified support from such religious groups as the American Lutheran Church and the United Methodist Board of Church and Society. Soon, four states had eased access to legal abortions.

In 1972, the U. S. Supreme Court ruled in favor of abortion rights activists, deciding in its landmark case *Roe v. Wade* that the Constitution prohibits interference by states in medical decisions between a woman and her physician during the first trimester of a pregnancy. In the later stages of a pregnancy, the court ruled, states could regulate abortion.

The reaction to the *Roe v. Wade* decision was immediate and galvanized a number of groups against access to abortion. The Catholic Church in America issued a statement that its members would be excommunicated if they participated in or received an abortion. Many Christian evangelical groups condemned the ruling as well, claiming that the Supreme Court had rejected morality. The anti-abortion movement, now referring to itself as pro-life, also gained strength and numbers among political conservatives during this period and into the 1980s. Abortion clinics became battlegrounds for the fight between pro-life and pro-choice (those supporting access to abortion) groups.

## Critical Overview

When *Backlash* was published in the fall of 1991, it was a popular success and stayed at the top of the *New York Times* bestseller list for months. Numerous critics praised Faludi for her use of compelling data and for the book's timely topic. Wendy Kaminer, writing in the *Atlantic,* called the book a "comprehensive survey of a powerful ten-year backlash against feminism." Faludi's critique of the media's role in maintaining this backlash, according to Kaminer, was "powerful," and she rejected some critics' accusations that the book was based on conspiracy theory. Kaminer, however, did warn readers that Faludi's work was much more descriptive than analytic.

Gayle Greene's review of Faludi's book in the *Nation* was similarly receptive, calling the book a "rich compendium of fascinating information and an indictment of a system." Greene also lauded Faludi's considerable interviewing skills and expressed surprise that the author was able to get her subjects to "blurt out marvelously self-incriminating revelations, offering up the real reasons they hate and fear feminists."

This praise continued in the *Whole Earth Review,* in which Ann Norton admired Faludi's book for its clarity and logical arguments. Norton also appreciated Faludi's use of specific examples in popular culture to drive home her points, making her book accessible to everyone interested in the topic. "This is the book for those who have puzzled and despaired ... over magazine and newspaper articles and TV news shows declaring the 'death of feminism,'" remarked Norton.

Not all of the reviews were positive however; Karen Lehrman, writing in the *New Republic,* argued that despite the large number of examples, Faludi's assigning malevolent and organized motives to the backlash was the book's undoing. She called Faludi's arguments "dubious" and accused Faludi of seeing "a cabal of villains ... successfully intimidating a large class of victims: women." Lehrman complained that Faludi's book portrayed women as victims until the very end, where the author admitted that woman have not been totally beaten by the backlash. "Writing this in the introduction would have undermined her portrayal of women as helpless, passive victims of society's devious designs," Lehrman asserted.

Some of the criticism of Faludi's book became quite vehement. Maggie Gallagher, writing for the *National Review,* called Faludi's book "an ignorant, nasty, little book ... small-minded, crafty, conniving, a disgrace even to journalistic standards, and an insult to women." She pointed to what she claimed was Faludi's misrepresentation of the facts in a number of instances, asserting that "evidence is not Miss Faludi's strong point." Gretchen Morgenson, writing in *Forbes,* condemned the book for shoddy reporting, bad writing, paranoia, and for encouraging women to think of themselves as victims. "In the opinion of this career woman," wrote Morgenson, " *Backlash* is a last gasp of Seventies feminism, a final attempt to rally women to a shrill, anti-male cause that has been comatose for years."

Some critics, while not agreeing with all of Faludi's arguments and methods, still realized the importance of the book. Nancy Gibbs, writing for *Time,* declared that the success of Faludi's book was based on "the resonance of the questions Faludi raises." While Gibbs admitted that Faludi did mishandle some statistics in her book, this "should not be an excuse to dismiss her entire argument." Faludi had, according to Gibbs, inspired both men and women to rethink how they relate to each other, on a personal as well as on a public level.

# What Do I Read Next?

- *Stiffed: The Betrayal of the*

*American Man* is Susan Faludi's second book, published in 1999. In this work, she furthers her studies in gender relations, chronicling the thoughts and words of post—World War II men.

- Simone de Beauvoir's groundbreaking 1953 book, *The Second Sex,* uses history, philosophy, economics, and biology to understand women's roles in the second half of the twentieth century. This book was published well before much thought was given to issues surrounding women's place in the world, and was one of the first books to discuss post—World War II feminism.

- *The Reader's Companion to U.S. Women's History* is a collection of four hundred articles celebrating the role of lesser-known women who have had an impact on American history. Wilma Mankiller, Gwendolyn Mink, Marysa Navarro, and Gloria Steinem edited the collection, published in 1999. Entries include an essay on the role of Native American women and a narrative on the female slave experience.

- American writer Grace Paley has

described herself as a pacifist, feminist, and anarchist. Her short stories include characters struggling to understand their roles in a society that often limits behavior based on gender. *The Collected Stories,* published in 1995, brings together more than thirty years of her acclaimed stories.

# Sources

Gallagher, Maggie, Review of *Backlash: The Undeclared War against American Women,* in *National Review,* Vol. 44, No. 6, March 30, 1992, pp. 41ff.(2).

Gibbs, Nancy, "The War against Feminism in Popular Culture, in Politics," in *Time,* Vol. 139, No. 10, March 9, 1992, p. 50.

Gibbs, Nancy, and Jeanne McDowell, "How to Revive a Revolution: Interview with Gloria Steinem and Susan Faludi," in *Time,* Vol. 139, No. 10, March 9, 1992, pp. 56ff.(2).

Greene, Gayle, Review of *Backlash: The Undeclared War against American Women,* in *Nation,* Vol. 254, No. 5, February 10, 1992, pp. 166ff.(5).

Kaminer, Wendy, Review of *Backlash: The Undeclared War against American Women,* in *Atlantic Monthly,* Vol. 268, No. 6, December 1991, pp. 123ff.(4).

Lehrman, Karen, Review of *Backlash: The Undeclared War against American Women,* in *New Republic,* Vol. 206, No. 11, March 16, 1992, pp. 30ff.(5).

Morgenson, Gretchen, "A Whiner's Bible," in *Forbes,* Vol. 149, No. 6, March 16, 1992, pp. 152ff. (2).

Norton, Ann, Review of *Backlash: The Undeclared War against American Women,*" in *Whole Earth Review,* No. 75, Summer 1992, p. 110.

# Further Reading

Bloom, Allan, *The Closing of the American Mind,* Touchstone Books, 1988.

> In this book, University of Chicago professor Allan Bloom expounds on the failings of the American education system. He argues that the social and political crisis of twentieth-century America is truly an intellectual crisis. Some feminists have criticized this book for a dismissive attitude toward women and their professional roles.

Bly, Robert, *Iron John: A Book about Men,* Vintage Books, 1992.

> Poet and former anti-war activist Robert Bly was one of the leaders of the men's movement in the 1980s, in which men were encouraged to rediscover their masculinity. This book was one of the critical texts of the movement, providing an examination of what it means to be a man through the story and adventures of the mythical Iron John.

Douglas, Susan J., *Where the Girls Are: Growing Up Female with the Mass Media,* Times Books, 1995.

> Susan Douglas has written an analysis of the effects of mass media on American women in the second half of the twentieth century. The book combines hard facts with humor.

Friedan, Betty, *Life So Far,* Simon and Schuster, 2000.

> Betty Friedan's autobiography covers her life from her beginning as a labor reporter to her work in founding the National Organization for Women and her work and writings since then.

Gilder, George, *Wealth and Poverty,* Institute for Contemporary Studies, 1993.

> This is George Gilder's most well-known book. Considered by conservatives to be a masterpiece, it discusses how to increase wealth and reduce poverty—but many feminists and liberal readers look upon it as a broadside against women's economic roles. Gilder argues that most welfare programs only serve to extend poverty and create victims dependent upon government programs.

CPSIA information can be obtained
at www.ICGtesting.com
Printed in the USA
BVHW042146250321
603490BV00015B/434